PLANET ZOO: CONSOLE EDITION

Guide and Walkthrough: Tips and Tricks To Play Better

CONTENTS

Tips and Tricks 1
- Beginner's tips and tricks for becoming the ultimate zookeeper 1
- Tips we swear by - how to make the best zoo ever 4
- Tips I wish I would've known sooner 7
- Tips for building an awesome animal prison 13

Getting Started 17
- Building Tips For Beginners 17
- Tips For Any New Player 23
- Top 10 Things To Pay Most Attention To 26
- Beginner's Tips For Building From Scratch 30
- A Beginners Guide To Habitats, Exhibits And Animal Care 41

Guides 45
- Maintaining Animal Welfare While Maximizing Profit 45
- Tips For Timed Scenarios 49
- Guide To Creating The Perfect Penguin Enclosure 52
- Tips For Breeding Perfect Animals 55
- Pro Tips Every Player Should Know 59
- How To Build A Hard Shelter 63
- How To Install And Use Mods 65

FAQ Guide 68

TIPS AND TRICKS

BEGINNER'S TIPS AND TRICKS FOR BECOMING THE ULTIMATE ZOOKEEPER

Play the campaign

Though it may be tempting to dive straight into Franchise or Sandbox mode to build the zoo of your dreams, the campaign and timed scenarios are a great way to learn all sorts of skills you need to call upon.

From the very basics, like raising enclosure fences and ensuring your animals have access to clean water, to the more advanced, the campaign is the perfect guide to begin your journey—and there are some fantastic buildings and designs you can take inspiration from.

Start small

Animals like elephants are likely at the top of your list in *Planet Zoo* for creatures you want to add to your zoo, but the best tactic is to start small and build from there. After all, if you were opening a zoo in real life, you probably wouldn't start with the largest land mammal in the world.

Aardvark's, Ostriches, and Warthogs are great options to start off with, along with the added bonus of getting Species Enrichment if paired in an enclosure with other animals (more on that later), and it isn't expensive to build the perfect environment for any of them.

Avoid large carnivores early on

Similarly to the above, lions and tigers may be among the most eye-catching and famous animals you want to add to your zoo in *Planet Zoo*, but they are also the most costly. In *Planet Zoo*, feeding carnivores is a lot more expensive than feeding the non-meat eaters.

Adding a large carnivore to your zoo too early can quickly deplete your funds and leave you with your back against the wall, struggling to make ends meet, so I highly recommend steering clear until you are much more established.

✦ Make use of the Workshop

Planet Zoo has a staggering amount of build items you can use to create your own buildings, shelters, and anything else you can think of, though it can also be daunting. If, like me, you're not the most creative player, the Planet Zoo Workshop is the place for you.

In the Workshop, you can save and download designs created by other players to add to your zoo. Just be careful in Franchise mode, as you need to have researched all the specific parts included in the build to place it.

✦ Buy animals for cash

There are two forms of currency in *Planet Zoo*, with cash being the primary one and the most easy to make, while the other is Conservation Credits—which are earned by selling animals on the marketplace or releasing them to the wild.

Conservation Credits are an extremely valuable resource in *Planet Zoo* and should be saved for the very best animals with high genetics, rare patterns, or ones that are just overly expensive. As such, don't use your Conservation Credits early on when adding basic animals.

The downside, however, is that animals purchased with cash cannot be later released in the wild to earn Conservation Credits. Instead, use them as your breeding animals and release the offspring.

✦ Don't forget Donation Boxes

Cash is king in Planet Zoo, and while entrance tickets, merchandise, and food may seem like the primary money makers, Donation Boxes can single-handedly drive your zoo to success—so don't forget to place them.

As a general rule, you should add at least one Donation Box per enclosure and should position the Donation Box in an area where guests have the best view of the animals. You can also use Education items in the area to increase the donation amounts.

Pay attention to social requirements

Once you have built the perfect enclosure in *Planet Zoo*, there are many animal requirements that won't vary. Social requirements, however, fluctuate regularly, so you keep a very close eye on this.

Each animal has a social requirement, which is how many adult animals can be in a group, and it's easy to tick over the threshold when baby creatures grow up. Similarly, more guests can result in higher foot traffic around an enclosure, increasing stress.

You can always stop animals from breeding by using contraceptives, or trade the offspring away for Conservation Credits, and use one-way glass on exhibit walls to reduce the stress.

Always research

When playing in Franchise, the Campaign, or Timed Scenarios, not all items are available immediately and have to be researched. When adding a new animal to your zoo, be sure to start vet research immediately.

Similarly, mechanic research is extremely beneficial as it unlocks one-way glass, more buildings, stronger fences, and more.

To get the best out of research, you can have one vet and a mechanic at your zoo who are solely dedicated to the research and do not complete any other tasks.

Use work zones

As your zoo grows, the number of employees on your payroll increases, too, and it can be easy to lose track. Once your zoo is big enough, it can be a mess trying to ensure everything gets the attention it needs—but work zones are the solution.

Using work zones, you can divide up areas of your zoo and assign workers to dedicate themselves to those zones—just make sure you include a Staff Room in the work zone so that your workers can get a well-deserved rest.

- **Read the Zoopedia**

Planet Zoo's Zoopedia is full of vital information on animals. The Zoopedia details their requirements, biome, continent, and other useful tidbits of information, including what other species they can be paired with to gain an enrichment bonus.

When designing a new enclosure, make sure to check out the Zoopedia to find out the minimum size required for the animal you want to add, as well as whether they need areas for swimming or climbing.

- **TIPS WE SWEAR BY - HOW TO MAKE THE BEST ZOO EVER**

- **Make sure to work through the Career mode first**

A lot – although not all – of the biggest questions I had about building a zoo are answered by playing through the Planet Zoo Career Mode. There are definite gaps in its tutorials, but it will run through the important things like how to make your animals happy, create basic habitats, and keep your critters healthy is all covered in there. It's just when it gets more complicated you might want a Planet Zoo tip or two.

- **Start with the easier, smaller animals**

Although you might think it's best to start with the big-ticket animals when starting your zoo, they are usually the highest maintenance residents with high enrichment and social requirements that you won't be able to meet straight away. Instead, start small and simple, with animals like ostriches, warthogs, and tortoises, which are all easy to maintain and will earn you Conservation Credits, and money to build more things in your zoo to bring in even more guests.

- **Buy animals for cash to begin with**

Conservation Credits are a little bit like gold dust in Planet Zoo, so it's easier to focus on the animals you can buy for cash money to begin with. That way, you can get them in cheaply, and they can start earning for you without you having to sacrifice the Credits you'll need for the biggest purchases later. Don't get greedy with the Grizzlies okay?

- **You can't trade animals you bought with money for Conservation Coins**

Although you can buy animals for money, it means that they're basically useless when you release them to the wild, in terms of earning you precious Planet Zoo Conservation Credits. Instead, turn your acquired critters into your breeding pair, and set their offspring lose to the wild for Credits instead. Yes, this might make your zoo sound like a breeding business, but it's the best way of getting everything you want.

- **Don't forget to place donation boxes**

Money, money, money. How can your guests show how much they appreciate your zoo unless you give them buckets to chuck their spare change into? Make sure you place enough Planet Zoo donation boxes for your guests to appreciate you, and boost your zoo's revenue funds.

- **Make sure to hire enough keepers and mechanics**

Although Planet Zoo caretakers and vets are obviously important, it's the keepers and mechanics that will keep your critters safe, fed, clean, and happy. Planet Zoo mechanics will maintain your habitats and make sure there aren't any escape risks, and Planet Zoo keepers will do everything animal related – namely clean up their poop, fill water and food troughs, and bring them new friends from the trading centre.

The game will tell you that you need to build all the staff facilities immediately when starting a new park, but actually you can get away with just the following:

- Trade Centre
- Staff Room
- Quarantine
- Keeper Hut

You can then have enough to get your zoo up and running, trading in the smaller animals, which will earn you enough money through guests to fund the other staff facilities a little later. It's a good way to save money in the short term.

A merchandise shop is a great way to please your guests

Toys, balloons, a novelty eraser? Everyone wants some merch, so why not give the people what they want by placing a Planet Zoo merchandise shop as your first port of call? They always say exit through the gift shop, after all. It'll bring in enough dosh to make sure you can give them the things that might also keep them alive. Namely, toilets, food and water. But first, the merch!

Watch how many male animals you have

If you have happy critters, they're going to start making some of their own to add to your zoo. That's obviously a great thing because a) baby animals are the cutest b) they can be raised and released into the wild for Conservation Coins and zoo reputation and c) pull in more guests. But, beware. If you have more than one male adult animal per enclosure they'll start fighting for alpha status, which means injuries, vet bills, and unhappy guests.

Don't be afraid to use contraception

If you're struggling to keep a Planet Zoo population at a manageable state, then don't be afraid to add some contraceptives to your animals' dinner. You can just slide across the toggle in the animal tab to add or remove contraceptives, at least until you've got your monkey problem under control.

- **Take advantage of the Steam Workshop blueprints**

If you don't want to be that creative yourself when it comes to building a zoo from scratch, you can root through the Planet Zoo Steam Workshop blueprints to discover what the community has already created. There's a raft of beautiful habitat, exhibit and other designs that already exist and can just be dropped straight into your zoo.

TIPS I WISH I WOULD'VE KNOWN SOONER

Planet Zoo tips for keeping your animals – and sanity – intact:

- From time to time, **other players' avatars** will come visit your zoo. Big tip: this isn't just for show! It's super easy to overlook, but you can actually earn conservation credits – a coveted resource used to get new animals from the Animal Market – just by saying hi to these VIPs. Whenever you see a **"visiting player"** alert on the left-hand side of the UI, click it, and then you'll get a prompt to greet them. Your reward? 20 credits!

- Note: you'll need to have an online connection to see visiting players, and there's a daily limit on how many conservation credits you can pile up this way. It's worth the trouble.

- You can also get credits from **daily logins**. Click "Franchise" from the main menu.

- If it seems like there's a way to **visit other zoos**, well, there isn't – not really. Your best bet is to take a look at the Steam Workshop where users can upload their custom-made items, many of which are as detailed as the official assets. I'd love for Frontier Developments to implement a hassle-free system that lets players tour zoos up-close.

- You can **add cool-looking windows** to your wood, brick, and concrete walls (just to name a few). To do so, click on a wall or habitat, then hit "edit barrier," and look near the bottom right of your screen for a "Window" option. From here, you can toggle glass windows on and off, and – once researched by Mechanics – even use one-way glass.

- As for **making barriers climb-proof**, many walls are inherently resistant to would-be climbers (you can hover your mouse over a barrier type to see this info). But for habitat barriers like Wood Logs, one of my personal favorite designs, you can stop animals from climbing out by heading into the "edit barrier" menu, clicking on the right-hand tab found toward the bottom of your screen, and selecting one of the "Climb Proof" options. Just be sure to choose the correct direction (pick "both" if you're unsure).

- Do you prefer **building paths on a grid**? Same! And there's a way to do in *Planet Zoo*. First, with the path-laying tool open, you'll want to click "Align to Grid" at the bottom of your screen – doing so will give your cursor a blue grid. You'll then need to click on an existing path or building in your zoo to sample it as a point of reference. Once you do that, you're free to plop down perfectly-spaced paths to your heart's content.

- Want a more believable-looking zoo? You can make **elevated pathways and stairs** using the keyboard shortcuts "u" and "j" to raise/lower a pathway while the path building tool is active. Alternatively, you can click to lay down a path, continue holding the left mouse button down, and drag your mouse up to raise the walkway.

- Okay, so say you made an ugly walkway. Say you want to get rid of all the evidence and take out the witnesses. How do you go about that? **To delete a path**, open up the path tool (from the bottom) and just click "Delete Path" – you can then erase by clicking.

- Bonus tip: you can **remove water** much the same way (or by clicking your scroll wheel).

- Are you getting a **"terrain modification failed"** error when you try to place paths? This was driving me nuts too. Try turning off the "Flatten Terrain" and "Tunneling" toggles inside the path-laying menu. If you *still* can't make new paths that connect to your existing ones, try deleting the original path and starting again with those options off.

- There's a trick to get your **barriers/fences to sit nicely near your paths**. The toggle is called "Snap Alongside Barriers" and it's located in the path tool, so open that up. You'll then need to click the right-hand tab and scroll down the list to find the option.

- Okay, just a few more control tips: you can painlessly decrease/increase the size of the terrain painter and the terrain sculptor using the bracket keys, [and] respectively.

- You can also **raise/lower objects** by holding the shift key while moving them around. This is so helpful for larger structures that are comprised of multiple smaller pieces (like caves made of rocks) or getting trees to sit in your zoo at variable heights.

- Also, if you want fine control over objects when rotating them, hold the Z key.

- There's a vital HUD element that'll be way too easily overlooked by anyone who skips the tutorial in *Planet Zoo*'s Career mode. See the **radar button** in the bottom left-hand corner? Learn it. Love it. Clicking the radar will give you access to lots of valuable info. You can see temperature heat maps, water quality, areas with (and without) electricity, details on how your staff buildings are negatively impacting guests, and more.

- If it seems as if items like **education boards, speakers, and benches are constantly breaking down**, hire more Security guards. (Also, you'll need to replace them.) I discovered this tidbit after watching a teen stomp on one of my benches. The little jerk!

- If you're the type of person who reads guides before buying a game to get a feel for it, first: *me too*! Second: here's an image of all the animals in *Planet Zoo*. (Note: the pygmy hippo, Thomson's gazelle, and Komodo dragon are Deluxe Edition exclusives.)

- To earn more conservation credits (and to feel better about yourself), consider **breeding and releasing critically endangered species**: the Bornean orangutan, Chinese pangolin, gharial, Himalayan brown bear, Lehmann's poison frog, Lesser Antillean iguana, red ruffed lemur, West African lion, western chimpanzee, and western lowland gorilla.

- It's possible to breed an albino baby, but it's up to chance. There's even an achievement.

- If you're wondering **what size a habitat should be**, it depends on the species. Find their Zoopedia file and click the "Natural Habitat" tab for exact details about their land, water, climbing, and temperature needs. (Speaking of, don't forget heaters and coolers.)

- To figure out the size of a habitat before you transfer any animals, click on the habitat you want to inspect and tab over to "Terrain" – you'll see the land and water area.

- How do you know **which plants to use in a habitat**? Click on an animal, switch to their "Environment" tab, and note the specific Continents and Biomes listed here. Now, go into the "Nature" menu (found at the bottom of the screen) and use the filter button to show only those Continents and Biomes. Note: this isn't 100% foolproof.

- If a plant is ill-suited, after you plop it down, you'll see a little red warning symbol in your animal's "Environment" tab. You can remove them right from this menu by clicking the red X.

- What about **food, water, and enrichment items**? The latter require Vet research for each species (though certain items overlap). Once again, filtering is your best bet.
- Click on the "Habitat" button at the bottom of the screen, then filter by species. *Done!*
- How do you make more money? Well, if you're just starting out, **don't bite off more than you can chew**. Make a single habitat, get your animals situated, and have your Veterinarians research the species so that you can add the appropriate enrichment toys and feeders.
- Education matters too. Vet research goes hand in hand with **increasing your education rating** and your guests' willingness to donate money (the primary source of income).
- You'll want to make ample use of the **Conservation Education Board** (throughout your zoo), the **Exhibit Education Board** (near exhibits), the **Habitat Education Stand** (near habitats), and **Educational Speakers** (all over). And Donation Boxes, of course.
- I'd also strongly discourage building Food and Drink stalls while your zoo is still getting off the ground. They're pricey to construct, and Vendor wages quickly add up. That said, I *would* consider building an Information Center – they sell umbrellas and audio guides.
- **Don't neglect habitat walls!** They'll deteriorate over time – especially if you play *Planet Zoo* at high speed – and your critters will cause a ruckus. Here are a few pointers.
- If you select a habitat, you can then click "Call Mechanic" to fix it up. Easy peasy.
- Or you can click on a habitat, swap to the right-most tab ("Maintenance"), and change the "Routine Visits" option from "Once a year" to something more regular.

- If you have a bunch of habitats, you might want a summary. Click the "Zoo" button on the bottom left of the screen, then mouse over to the "Animals" page, then switch to the "Habitats" tab. Got me? Good. From here, you'll see how every habitat barrier is doing, and you can click on the little destination icon to pull up individual habitat pages.
- Is an animal's **Nutrition rating** lower than you'd like? You may want to bump up your food quality. The more you research a species (with Vets), the better food you'll be able to produce, but there's more to it – you have to manually change the meal plan.
- Click on a habitat, then switch to the "Animals" tab, and change the food quality from Grade 1 to Grade 2 or Grade 3. If you don't have these options yet, you need to do more research. The higher the grade, the pricier the food, so don't go bankrupting yourself.
- Unlike other tycoon games, you can't manually feed animals or clean habitats.
- If your **keepers aren't feeding animals properly**, it's worth explaining their behavior, because it can seem nonsensical. "Keepers will work out how much food they need to prepare for a habitat based on how many animals are in the habitat. They will then prioritize filling enrichment feeders before standard feeders. This can mean that if all of the prepared food is placed in enrichment feeders, the standard feeders won't be filled."
- If keepers aren't **cleaning habitats** well enough, you may want to promote your existing staff or bring on some fresh faces to help out. You can increase a staff member's rating by opening the Zoo menu (at the bottom of the screen), going to the "Staff" tab, and putting your cursor next to an employee's star rating. You'll see a little arrow appear.

- Too many bundles of joy? Take a chill pill. **You can give your animals contraceptives.** Click on the "Zoo" button at the bottom, then head to the "Animals" tab. On the far right, there's a "Contraception" toggle. Note: you can reverse this at any time.

- There's a **Zoopedia shortcut** to save you from having to scroll down the usual list. Click on an animal in your zoo to bring up their welfare summary. Now, look for this icon:

- **Selling and trading animals** in *Planet Zoo* is a two-step process. First, locate the animal, click on them to bring up their summary, and look for a "Send animal to storage in Trade Centre" button below the "Call Vet" and "Call Keeper" buttons. Click it!

- Next, open up the Animal Trading menu (it's on the bottom of the screen, right above your zoo's money) and head to the "Animal Storage" tab. From here, you'll be able to **trade** or **release to the wild** for conservation credits, or **quick trade** for cold hard cash.

- Note: you can't ditch your juveniles/infants. You'll need to raise your animals until they reach adulthood/sexual maturity before selling them off.

TIPS FOR BUILDING AN AWESOME ANIMAL PRISON

Remap 'pause' to the spacebar

By default the spacebar is mapped to the 'angle snap' toggle, but trust me, you're going to want to pause the game more often than you do just about anything else. Even on the slowest setting, time passes deceptively quickly. If you let the game run while you spend 10 or 15 minutes crafting a habitat, you might find dozens of babies have been born, adult animals have died of old age, or other issues have cropped up. Get in the habit of pausing often, and tapping the spacebar is the most natural way to do it.

Start slow and think small

My impulse was to build a habitat, drop a pair of animals into it, make sure they were happy-ish, and then immediately begin building another habitat to expand my zoo just as quickly as I could. But it takes quite a bit of time to start seeing profits match your efforts, and if you build and expand too quickly you're going to sink quickly into a money pit. Every habitat and exhibit takes a surprising amount of resources to keep running.

So take your time. Start small, and only expand when you're making a profit or at least just breaking even. Don't build too much, adopt too many animals or hire too much staff. Check your budget tab regularly to see where you're making money and where you're losing it, too.

You can add windows to walls

You can build solid walls to keep animals in their habitats, and glass walls so people can gawk at them, but solid walls with windows built into them look much nicer (and somehow feel more realistic) than just a big blank pane of glass. There's an easy-to-miss option to add windows to solid walls (scroll down a tad in the box on the lower right) that allows you to build windows into brick and wooden walls.

You can make animals immortal in sandbox mode

As someone who has accidentally allowed animals to starve to death, contract diseases, and sustain horrible injuries, let me tell you: it's heartbreaking. If you play on sandbox mode you can turn all that off. Obviously it's not realistic, but it might make you happier. And while your human staff members don't age and die, they do sometimes quit. You can turn that off too, and force them to work for eternity in your immortal, undying zoo.

You can game the bronze objectives in career mode

Completing the first series of objectives (bronze) in career mode unlocks the zoo and map in challenge and sandbox modes. That lets you move onto the next career mode zoo. The nice thing is that once you've satisfied any bronze goal, it's considered done forever, even if you immediately begin failing that goal a moment later.

Example: in one career mode zoo, there was a bronze goal for my zoo to make a profit and another goal to get my employee happiness over 70%. These are hard to accomplish at the same time without lots of balancing and tweaking. So I just lowered the employees' pay to rock bottom until my profits satisfied the first goal, then immediately cranked their pay up to the max to make the employees happy.

Even though overpaying my employees plunged me into negative profits, it didn't matter because I'd already accomplished the profit goal first. Obviously this doesn't work if you want to continue the career mode to achieve the silver and gold goals for that zoo, but for unlocking the map quickly for use in other modes or for moving onto the next career mode zoo, it works just fine.

Shared habitats are good for everyone

If you're looking to save money on construction costs and get a lot of value from less land, acquire animals that can share their habitats with different species. Giraffes, buffaloes, warthogs, gazelles, and many others are actually happier occupying the same habitats with certain other species—the in-game Zoopedia will tell you with whom they benefit from living. It's easier for your staff to manage these animals when they're all together instead of spread out all over the place and it makes it clearer for your guests to see and learn about different animals without getting tired from walking too far. And the animals like each other. Win-win-win.

Your employees need separate habitats, though

If you've ordered a mechanic or vet to do research or a zookeeper to handle some important task, you may wind up waiting a long time, and it's not always obvious why. Your staff members may be bottlenecked because they can't simultaneously use small facilities. While one zookeeper is chopping up food, or a mechanic is studying new zoo technology, anyone else will have to wait patiently outside, peering in through the window if it's the only small facility available. (Research can unlock larger facilities that can be shared by more than one employee.)

It might also be down to guest congestion. If your employees are slow getting around, think about building them their own dedicated staff paths so they don't bump into guests.

- **Guests love buying dumb hats**

Raising admission fees for a small zoo will draw complaints. Food and drink stalls are hit and miss. People, shockingly, don't like paying to use the toilets. Donation boxes placed outside habitats are great earners, but your guests still typically leave your zoo with hundreds of unspent dollars in their pockets. How can you drain it from them?

Big dumb hats. Balloons, too, but mostly, big dumb animal hats. Before you even start putting in Chief Beef burger huts and drink stalls, get souvenir shops researched and make sure everyone can buy a big dumb hat. They will, in droves.

- **You can adjust how quickly you need to pay back loans**

Making a profit with your zoo is hard—and it's the kind of hard where I'm honestly expecting a post-launch patch to make it a bit easier. At the moment, though, loans can help keep you afloat, and you can adjust the monthly repayments from the loan menu.

I'm not really advising you do this, because I've currently got a $50,000 loan on my park that is going to cost me over $215,000 to pay back over the next, um, 34 years. But the point is, if you take out a loan, you can adjust how long you want to take to pay it back, which can help you out with lower payments in the short term even if it doesn't do you any real favors in the long term.

- **You can kick people out of the zoo**

Some of your guests will be dicks. There may be vandals, litterbugs, and even pickpockets hiding among the nice people who just want to look at your zebras and giant snails. I've never specifically spotted anyone doing something wrong, but if you do you can sic a security guard on them and kick them out. Or, you can just do it for fun. Just make sure they buy a hat first. This goes for individuals or groups, though, not protesters.

- **If you split a habitat, move the gate first**

When building habitats I tend to err on the side of caution. So if the Zoopedia tells me a western lowland gorilla needs 780 meters of space, I'll overcompensate and build a habitat that's got, like, 2,900 meters of space. I just don't want to risk my gorilla being unhappy, you know? But later I'll need to find room for other animals so I'll want to divide that habitat up a bit.

It's easy enough to draw some barriers through the middle and turn that huge habitat into two smaller ones. But before doing that, make sure the gate winds up in the same section the habitat's current resident is in. If you divide a habitat in half and the animal is in one half but its gate is in the other, Planet Zoo will decide the animal has escaped. Even if it's just sleeping peacefully as the bear in the above image is.

GETTING STARTED

BUILDING TIPS FOR BEGINNERS

Start By Building In Sandbox Mode

One of the best ways to learn how to build is to **jump into sandbox mode**. Here you don't need to worry about finances or goals and you can just learn the basics with no pressure. The 1.6 update also enhanced sandbox so its easier to build your dream zoo thanks to the **disabling of most negative effects**. Overcrowding, animal stress, fights, fear, animal escapes, negative guest happiness, stale food and dirty water are all off my default. This means fiddling with settings you don't quite understand is a thing of the past as by default your zoo should run much smoother.

While you can **start totally from scratch**, it's actually **easier to begin with an existing scenario zoo**. This is because you have examples to work with and copy.

The **very first scenario zoo** is ideal for learning the basics of building. This is because it contains a **half-built custom shop area** that you can simply edit and adjust. It's also a **functioning zoo** so if you want to see how your buildings work with customers, everything is already up and running. There are a **few minor adjustments** you can make to the **existing exhibits,** especially regarding foliage, and **hiring a few extra staff means fewer management issues**, but generally, the zoo is fine as it is.

By the **zoo entrance and exit** are **two brick buildings with shops in**. If you click on one of these you can **choose to edit the structure.** You can now click on individual pieces and see how they fit together. This building is basic in terms of pieces it uses but still looks great. The basic pieces you'll discover in buildings are:

- Foundations
- Walls of differing heights
- Walls with gaps for doors and windows
- Roof tiles
- Roof trim
- Accent pieces

Spending some time **moving things around to see how they join together** helps you learn how to structure buildings but basically you can **add a shop shell and then build around it**, making sure to check you use pieces that contain gaps wherre the doors and windows are.

↳ **How To Add Shops To An Existing Building**

Once you've figured out how things go together you can try adding stores into the building. There's a ready-made gap next to the Loony Bloons store and a store will fit into this space. To place it first find the store you want and choose the basic shop with no fancy decor. Then click the main building to add the shop to the structure.

As a default, the shops want to link to a path. As such the store should fit easily into this space with no adjustments needed. However, if you do need to adjust them keyboard shortcuts are the trick.

These handy tricks will help you adjust the buildings:

- **Holding shift** allows you to **move items up and down** with the mouse and enables you to **place them at the right level** if they are trying to slot in higher or lower than the gap.
- You can also **press z** to **rotate a shop** if it wants to connect the wrong way.

Just using these keys can make a huge difference and mostly they will enable you to place stores into buildings. You can also try removing paths nearby if you still have trouble. Often replacing a path **resets the connection** and allows things to connect better.

You can also use these same tricks to add shops or small exhibits to the **pre-built shells you'll find in the facilities menu**. These allow you to theme your zoos easily without building too much and are the **first step to customization**. You can edit all the shells to **adjust or add little details** and make them feel like your own.

For instance, in the building above you simply need to **remove the wall where the Cosmic Cow shop is** and **duplicate the two-piece facade** that's in front of the Chief Beef store to replace it. The shop wants to connect to the path behind but **hitting z turns it around**. You can then use the **advance move tools** to place the shop signs.

The easiest way to get signs right is to **place them close by and then use the advanced move option.**

- Adjust each angle using the circles
- Get the sign close to your desired location
- Change the camera angle to check how it matches up to the building.

You can also use the **snapping options** to get them to line up with the walls with less effort. Different people will prefer different settings so feel free to fiddle with these and see which you prefer.

Building From Scratch In Planet Zoo

Behind the building we just edited, there is a patch of land great for testing out builds. However, you'll need to use a trick to get the paths to match up if you want a square path up to your new building.

You first need to **connect a regular path to the existing path as usual.** You'll see it place just off the existing path and you only need to place **one short piece.** You can then choose **select grid, tick square edges,** and **click on the path you just placed** to get its grid. You'll then be able to **create a path that matches up.**

If you click the path that's already placed as your grid the paths won't match up, as shown above. It's a weird terrain quirk and one that often frustrates players.

Once your space is ready it's time to start building.

Flooring

Placing flooring isn't essential but it can help you **arrange things in a grid shape** and you can always delete it later. You'll notice that **items you place on top of it will snap to the edges.** Long grass will also **poke through flooring** so it looks better if you **edit the terrain underneath it.**

Make sure when you add pieces that you **follow the prompts** if required to add them to the group. This makes life much easier as your building can then be **moved as one item**.

Walls

There are **different types of walls** and these fit with the items you'll need to build around. You'll find plain walls as well as those with gaps for doors, windows, and storefronts. Use the **shift key and mouse** to move walls up and down if required. **Clicking z** will rotate the pieces.

It's often easier to **build a basic shell** then add your buildings and restructure around them. All buildings are under facilities, while the individual building pieces are under construction.

Buildings

The buildings should **snap into place** but you may need to adjust them using shift to change the height, especially if you keep the flooring. The terrain underneath your building may adjust itself as you build but it will be covered so you don't need to worry too much.

Check the terrain looks ok around the building before you go too far as terrain is difficult to edit once it has a building on it.

If you need a path up to a walkway and it won't place the trick is to **add a building to the gap so the pathway automatically places** and then delete the building.

Roofs

Roofs are the **trickiest part** but thankfully there are usually **pre-built pieces that help**. The main thing you need to remember is **once you've selected the roof click the clipboard on the right-hand side and tick the box that says auto stacking.** This will allow the roof pieces to place on top of your structure by default. Then follow these steps.

- Start with the **corners first**
- Use **z and your mouse** to align each piece.

- You can then **add in the main roof pieces**.
- If pieces won't place simply **adjust the camera angle** a little and that should fix the issue.
- You can also **change the camera settings** in the options to be able to get into tighter spaces and see what you are doing.
- Experiment with **different settings** to see which feels easiest to use.

If you want to make the inside look a little neater you can **place a flat roof on top of your buildings directly** to neaten up the gaps.

Roof Edging

Placing roof edging is the **fiddliest part.** You'll need to **find theright pieces then hold down shift while moving them into place.** If they snap too high it can be easier to **take off object snapping** then move them up from the ground.

The easiest way to finish a basic roof is to **place flat pieces across the gap at the top and use the edging to neaten them up.** The process is fiddly but it's like a giant jigsaw and you will get faster as you build more frequently.

Most of the building process in Planet Zoo is simply trial and error. Don't be afraid to change settings, pull apart existing buildings, experiment with editing, and generally just get a feel for how things match together. It can take a while but once you've got a rhythm that works for you then you'll be able to adjust and create buildings in no time.

- **Finishing Touches**

The finishing touches are what will set your building apart. You can add signs, decals, lettering, and even statues. When adding lettering or decals to walls or signs checking the align to surface and position snap buttons will allow for easier placement.

The best way to build a beautiful building is **simply to experiment**. Every decorative item can be moved using the advance move tool so you can position things precisely. You can also add lighting to the area but it's a good idea to check how it looks by **adjusting the time of day** using the atmospheric conditions button while in build mode. This is because many of the lights are **very limited**.

As with everything in this game, taking your time and trying different things is key to learning to build. There's also a lot to be said for the speed of **pre-built shells and blueprints from the workshop** so don't be afraid to mix and match custom designs, shells, and blueprints together to create something truly unique.

If you want more help with your zoo planning make sure to check out our other Planet Zoo articles.

TIPS FOR ANY NEW PLAYER

Play The Tutorial In Career Mode First

It can be tempting to jump right into franchise mode to participate in the community challenge, but this will leave you hating the game in minutes. It is best to start in career mode with the tutorial section so you can learn what it has to offer, how to care for animals, and the different things you have at your disposal.

This will lessen the headache when you do move on to bigger and better things that require a more careful eye. You can even watch a few streamer tutorials before playing as well to understand the game and how to play.

Solar Panels Don't Cause Negative Reactions From Guests

You will quickly find out that things like staff buildings and transformers will have a negative impact on your guests. The best way to rid yourself of the headache involved with transformers is to upgrade your power supply in mechanical research until you have access to solar panels.

These have no impact on guests, which means they can be placed virtually anywhere, instead of hidden away in an obscure corner like a transformer. They are a bit more expensive, but the result is happier guests and a more self-sustaining zoo.

Assign Staff To Workzones

It is a common complaint that staff are not doing their intended jobs and prefer to wander around the zoo instead. The best way to prevent this from happening is to assign them to workzones.

YOu can make your entire zoo one big workzone, or you can make smaller workzones that are only for particular sections of the zoo or for certain staff members. Make sure you include a staff room in each workzone you create so you don't have members complaining that there is nowhere for them to rest due to your mistake.

Exhibit Animals Are The Perfect Start For Your Zoo

It might seem kind of pointless to start a zoo with a few tarantulas and snakes, but this is the best way to make money. It brings in guests, and if you splurge a bit more on those with a higher appeal, then you will notice an increase in profits.

These exhibit animals also reproduce quite quickly, and you can usually sell them for a decent amount of cash to help your zoo thrive. The first habitat animal you obtain should be one with the highest appeal to increase your guest's feelings about the zoo even further and you should focus on researching the animal before moving on to your second habitat.

Training Your Staff Helps A Lot

It is generally cheaper to train a staff member than to hire someone new. When you are first starting on your zoo, you should try to train the staff you have to help save you a few dollars.

All you have to is click on a staff member, toggle over to the education page for them, and pay the small fee to have them educated. They will begin to handle a bigger workload and it will decrease your need to hire another worker. Training them will increase their salaries, but it is a small amount that is worth a few extra dollars.

"X," "Z," And "Shift" Are Integral To Building

When you first start building it can be confusing how to move objects in different directions and on multiple axes. The "Z" key allows you to spin the object, which is the one players find the most useful.

If you want to become a little more advanced you can tap "X" once or twice and it will toggle advanced building where you can rotate objects in any direction to create more complicated structures. The "Shift" key allows you to raise or lower an object by holding it down and moving your mouse.

Stressed Animals Need Hiding Spots Or Ambiance Speakers

It is pretty common for certain animals to become stressed, especially as your guest count skyrockets. If you have added several hiding spots for your animal and it still proceeds to have low welfare due to stress, then consider adding ambiance speakers.

You can place these speakers inside of the exhibit and set them to the sounds the animal might hear in the wild. It will decrease their stress tremendously as the animal can tune out the noise that has been driving them crazy and bring their welfare up to a normal level.

Add A Staff Room Perk

When the staff is tired, they head over to the staff room to kick back and relax while they regain some energy. Many players fail to realize you can assign a perk that helps them become better at their job.

The perks do several things like lessen the chance they feel overworked, train them, increase guest happiness, and so much more. It will make a difference in your zoo depending on what perk you choose as it cuts down on different issues that happen to arise.

Enrichment Items Are Used For Multiple Species

When you research an animal, it is common for you to unlock an enrichment item for that species. Many new players fail to realize that this item is also good for other species in their zoo. The way you can tell is to click on the enrichment item, and on the right side of the lower menu is a tab that says "tags."

When you click on this it will bring up a list of animals that can use this item, so you are helping enrich more animals than just one. Your animals will be happier, and your guests will be happy that your animals are playing with new toys.

Donation Boxes Will Make Or Break Your Zoo

It might seem silly to place donation boxes when we all know that many of us don't have coins or cash to throw into them at our local zoos. Fortunately, the zoos in this game have guests whose pockets are overflowing with cash that they feel they need to throw in a donation box.

You should try and place them at every spot where guests stop to view an animal, and you can increase donations through education. Placing education boards and speakers will convince your guests they need to throw more money into the box. It brings in more cash than you think and will give you a jumpstart in your first zoo.

If you want more help with your zoo planning make sure to check out our other Planet Zoo articles.

TOP 10 THINGS TO PAY MOST ATTENTION TO

Visiting Players

While it may seem like visitors are just a gimmick, they actually offer a reward. If you click on the name of the player on the UI tab when you see visiting player notification then you'll be prompted to greet them. Doing so will award 20 conservation credits so it is well worth the effort.

Conservation credits can be used to purchase healthier and rarer animals and can be difficult to build up. This little trick will give you a nice boost over time, helping your zoo become more unique.

The Radar

The radar button is in the bottom left-hand corner of your screen and this will help you see any issues at a glance. It offers a range of heat maps for temperature, water quality, negative impact, electricity and more.

A frequent flick through these heat maps is the easiest way to spot issues before all the red warnings appear. Notifications tend to only kick in once things are dire. One to monitor early on is the negative effect on guests. Use this to ensure staff buildings are kept far enough from paths to minimize the impact on guest happiness.

Barrier Settings

At first glance, the barriers seem like a nightmare. Are they climbable, transparent, strong? It can appear that you have to compromise on something but in actual fact, most barriers are highly customizable.

If you click through both option tabs on the right side of the screen you'll notice that you can add glass windows and anti-climb barriers to almost any barrier. This is alongside the tools you'd expect to adjust height and length. You can also change the maintenance settings to ensure barriers are repaired more frequently.

Habitat Size

One of the easiest ways to build a suitable habitat is to build a basic barrier then put the animal inside and hit pause. Clicking an animal in a habitat will allow you to see exactly how you need to adjust it.

First, check the size, water, and climbing needs. Remember that if you want to breed animals you'll need to keep the size above the base to allow for extras. The first screen will show you the current size and how it compares to the ideals.

Animal Needs

Once the basic habitat is in place and suitably sized you can adjust other aspects to meet the animal's needs. As you adjust terrain, temperature, and foliage, these changes effects will show on the animal panel, even in pause.

Make sure you check your animal's preference for area and climate to get the correct foliage and don't forget food, water, and shelter as well as any basic enrichment you have.

Pathway Options

In certain zoos especially, paths can be tricky. The pathing tool is powerful but also annoying, especially for beginners. You can minimize issues by fiddling with some of the options.

Turning off the flatten terrain and tunnoling options can help avoid "terrain modification failed" errors. You can also use U and J or hold the left shift button to raise and lower paths to create inclines or stairs. If you've already built an enclosure, the snap alongside barriers option can help keep the path on track.

Staff Levels

Staff all play different roles and some perform duties you may not have considered. While mechanics repairing fences and vets treating sick animals is an obvious occurrence, the implications of security guards' roles are less so.

Without security, you may find benches break and education boards or speakers need more frequent repairs. This is because vandalism is the cause of many of these minor breakdowns and is alleviated with security. You won't need security immediately but it's a solid investment once your visitors are steady.

Vet Research

Vet research actually plays several roles in your zoo. The first important role is in animal welfare. As a default, you'll begin with only a few enrichment items. Vet research will help you gain more, allowing you to increase animal welfare by adding and rotating these in your exhibits.

A vets animal research also increases your education rating making education boards and speakers more valuable and prompting more donations. Finally, research into diseases helps keep animals healthy and treat sick animals more efficiently.

Mechanic Research

Mechanic research will help with new themes, power sources and staff facilities. All these can really help make your zoo more efficient. Larger staff buildings allow more staff to use them at one time while reducing space and power requirements.

Combine these facilities with staff promotions and new staff when needed to ensure your zoo is in good working order. Just remember that researching staff won't perform other duties at the same time.

Guest Happiness

Guests will have different specific needs but there are some basics you need to make sure you fulfill. Food and drink stands should be well spaced to cater for hunger and thirst, you'll also need restrooms for the after-effects. Alongside these benches to combat tiredness and bins to keep litter under control also help with happiness.

To increase revenue from your happy guests place ATMs near vendors or donation boxes and keep an eye on notifications about your zoo's price. Frequent education boards and speakers also help keep guests in a giving mood.

If you want more help with your zoo planning make sure to check out our other Planet Zoo articles.

⊥ BEGINNER'S TIPS FOR BUILDING FROM SCRATCH

⊥ Setting Up Your Staff Facilities

For this guide we're using **Maple Leaf Wildlife Park as our example**, but the advice is the same for any zoo you need to build from scratch. The only difference here is that **we begin this map with a Vet Surgery, Trade Centre, Small Staff Room, Quarantine, and Keeper Hut** already in place.

If you don't have these staff buildings, then you'll need them since **the heart of your zoo is the staff buildings**. Here's what you'll need and the function of each one.

The shell cost is just for the building itself and while it will function, it will have a negative effect on visitors in a larger radius. The building cost included here is for the base game default pre-built option.

⊥ Every Staff Building

Staff Building	Cost	Use
Animal Trade Centre	$1,000 - Shell	Animals are taken here after you purchase or adopt them.
	$1,370 - With Building	You cannot acquire animals without a Trade Centre.
Quarantine (Small)	$4,000 - Shell	Quarantine isolates animals and helps prevent disease spreading.

Staff Building	Cost	Use
	$5,065 - With Building	New animals should be quarantined on arrival to help prevent outbreaks of disease.
Veterinary Surgery	$4,000 - Shell	Sick animals are treated here.
	$5,005 - With Building	Vets will move any non-contagious animals here for treatment.
Keeper Hut (Small)	$1,000 - Shell	Animal food is prepared and collected here.
	$1,370 - With Building	Keepers will need to access these huts in order to distribute food to animals.
Staff Room (Small)	$2,000 - Shell	Staff can rest here.
	$2,490 - With Buildings	Staff need to rest, or they will work poorly and then quit.
Workshop	$1,000 -	Mechanics can do research here.

Staff Building	Cost	Use
	Shell	
	$1,380 - With Building	Mechanic research helps improve your infrastructure including: fences, paths, shops, facilities, and park themes.
Research Centre	$1,000 - Shell	Vets will perform research here.
	$1,370 - With Building	Vets will research animal care and enrichment items as well as uncover cures for common diseases.

You can manage without a Workshop and Research Centre initially, but you will want to **build a Research Centre early** on to help **maintain animal welfare**. Even level one animal research makes a huge difference, as it unlocks **vital enrichment items.**

Mechanic Research is less important in the early game, although this varies depending on your aim. **Extra shops will improve income,** and stronger fences will help reduce the chances of animal escape.

Staff Building Placement

It's recommended to place the **Animal Trade Centre, Vet Surgery, and Quarantine close together,** as animals will often be transferred between the three.

Staff Rooms and Keeper Huts are best placed in pairs around the zoo. A keeper having easy access to both of these buildings from all habitats or exhibits they will be in charge of helps them work more efficiently.

In this scenario, **adding the extra staff buildings just to the right of the existing ones** helps keep things together and looks much neater. However, you **don't have access to the wooden buildings,** so if you want to replicate them you'll need to **duplicate the existing ones** then edit them to fit the extras.

Your **Workshop and Research centre can go anywhere**, but we recommend **grouping them with the main buildings**. It allows vets to get to Quarantine or Surgery faster, and also **minimises the negative effects** of the building.

Setting Up Your Guest Facilities

There are **fewer required guest facilities**, but they are **equally vital at an early stage**, if not more so. If guests aren't provided for, then they will leave. **Guest facilities will keep them in the park**, and keep them spending and donating to your zoo.

Here are the main categories of guest facilities and their functions.

Every Guest Building

Guest Facility	Cost	Variants
Drink Stalls	$2,000 - Shell	Gulpee Soda - Gulpee Slush
	$2,335 - Gulpee Building	Gulpee Energy - Pipshot Water
		Pipshot Juice - Pipshot

Guest Facility	Cost	Variants
		Smoothies
		Street Fox Coffee - Cosmic Cow Milkshakes
Food Stalls	$2,000 - Shell $2,535 - Chief Beef Building	Chief Beef - Hotdog Squad Pizza Pen - Monsieur Frites Mexelente - Cosmic Cow Ice Cream Bernie's Bakes - Missy Good
Shops	$2,000 - Shell $2,535 - Info Centre Building	Information Center - Just A Momento Loony Blooons - Hat's Fantastic
Toilets	$2,000 - Small Shell $2,330 - Small Building	Small Building - Two Entrances Large Building - Four

Guest Facility	Cost	Variants
	$4,750 - Large Building	Entrances
Finance	$250 - ATM	ATM - Allows guests to withdraw cash
	$50.00 Donation Box	Donation Box - Collects guest donations

You can also get **vending machines and counters** for all food and drink stalls, except Bernie's Bakes, which doesn't have a vending machine. All shops (including Bernie's Bakes) have a counter option.

Vending machines are a cheap way to add extra food and drink options in areas which need it, since they just require occasional **refills from a mechanic, rather than a dedicated vendor.** However, they don't satisfy guests as much as the stalls do.

Guest Facility Placement

You'll want to have **at least one food and drink stall, as well as some toilets.** Ideally, these should be fairly central to an area of the park with a group of habitats and exhibits, so they are **easy to access.** As the park expands, include a second set in the new area.

If you have areas slightly out of the way due to the park terrain, add a small set of toilets and a couple of vending machines to help keep guests' needs up.

Every habitat and exhibit should also have a donation box near it. You'll want to add these to any viewing points, or areas where guests congregate. They are cheap, and you will collect a lot of money from them. **The happier guests are, the more they will donate.** To make them happy you should:

- **Increase animal welfare** - Happier animals make happier guests.
- **Prioritise high appeal animals when possible** - The more appealing the animal the more generous the guest.
- **Have good guest facilities in the area** - Guests who have access to food, drink and toilets are much happier.

It's also good to spread ATMs around, so guests can increase the money in their pockets and donate more of it to your zoo!

↓ **Negating The Negative Impact Of Buildings On Guests**

Staff facility buildings will have a negative impact on guests that pass by them. The image above shows two different sizes of staff building, both as a shell and with the default shell around them. As you can see, **the size of the red area is increased for buildings without any decor.**

To avoid negative impact on guests, the best way to **negate this negative effect** from your staff buildings is actually to add them in the same way the core facilities have been added to Mapleleaf Wildlife Park.

All staff buildings here are **together but set aside far enough from the main path that the red markers won't reach it.** Access to them is added using a **staff path**, which means guests won't walk along it.

Similarly, a great way to keep Keeper Huts and Staff Rooms away from guests is to **have a staff path running between enclosures and then add the staff buildings at the back**, with guest viewing access at the front.

↓ **Setting Up An Exhibit**

Exhibits are cheaper, smaller, and easier to set up than habitats, and they still keep the guests happy. A good zoo will require a **variety of animals**, but having a handful of exhibits dotted around a smaller zoo will help hold guest's interest.

A singular exhibit costs $3,000 for the shell or $3,800 with the basic building. You can also purchase the Medium Exhibit building, which holds two exhibit animals, for $7,065 or the Large Exhibit building, which holds four, for $13,700.

Once you've purchased an exhibit, you'll need to **head to the Exhibit Trading screen to purchase an exhibit animal** to inhabit it.

Exhibit animals start at just $100 or so and the vast majority are under $1,000 each. Exhibits also only have a running cost for power and food. **There are no extra costs for terrain, fauna etc.**

These will be added automatically to suit the animal, and you'll just need to **adjust the temperature and humidity.**

An exhibit will start at around **40% suitability** and this can be increased via research. Just remember to go into the **layout tab** of the exhibit to add newly researched items and increase this percentage.

Exhibit animals fill small gaps in the zoo and keep guests interested. **Each exhibit will be visible from multiple sides**, so you can minimise the crowding. More popular exhibits will need more viewing sites, so use smaller enclosures for these.

Setting Up A Habitat

Next, you'll need a **habitat animal to keep guests interested in your zoo** and fulfill the level criteria. When you are just starting out the **costs of both the animal itself, and creating its exhibit will make a difference.** Here are some things to look out for:

- **How much space do they need?** - A larger enclosure will cost more in fencing.

- **How much foliage do they need?** - The higher the percentage of foliage they need the more it will cost to meet it.
- **How large does the social group of animals need to be?** - More animals mean more cost.
- **How often do they reproduce?** - Offspring can be sold or released for cash or conservation credits so frequenty offspring can produce a source of income.
- **How much appeal do they have?** - Animals with a higher appeal will attract more guests and in turn more donations.

Balancing these things will help you keep your zoo in order as you add your habitat animals.

Hiring Staff

You'll need to **hire some staff to keep things running**. Here's what they all do:

All Staff

Staff Role	Starting Salary	Duties
Vet	$1,100 per month	Heal sick animals Relocate escaped animals Research animal care
Keeper	$1,000 per month	Feed animals Clean habitats and exhibits

Staff Role	Starting Salary	Duties
Educator	$1,000 per month	Give animal talks Run guided tours
Mechanic	$1,100 per month	Maintain and fix fences Maintain and repair facilities Stock vending machines Research park facilities
Security Guards	$1,100 per month	Prevent pick pocketing Prevent vandalism Help guests feel safe
Caretaker	$280 per month	Clean paths, toilets, benches Empty trash

Staff Role	Starting Salary	Duties
		Transport animals
Vendor	$230 per month	Serve in shops or stalls Serve on counters

You will need **one keeper per two habitats or four exhibits**. For other staff, **caretakers, security, guides, and mechanics** should be slowly increased with the size of the park. Have **at least one vet,** ideally two, if you want to keep research steady. You should also have **one extra vendor per three or so shops.**

Staff Management

The best way to balance staff is to **check the Staff List**. Here you can assign work zones to staff and also see how tired they are, how happy they are, and how much work load they have. This is **the easiest way to balance their needs and your park needs.**

- Adding All The Extras

You'll also need to make sure you **add in all the extras to keep things flowing**. These are:

- **Utilities** - Make sure you have clean water and power covering the park.

- **Paths** - Everything needs to be connected with a path. Staff paths will only allow staff to walk here, other paths will be used by guests.

- **Benches** - Make sure guests can sit. It's also good to add picnic benches near food stalls, but these need to be on a path.

- **Trash Cans** - The more you have, the less trash will be on the ground, ruining your zoo's appeal.

Good infrastructure is vital so think about where guests will walk.

A Checklist For Starting A Zoo

Here's what you need to do, in order, when starting a zoo.

- **Add Staff Facilities** - You can ignore workshop and research centre initially if you prefer. Make sure to connect them to each other and your main path with staff paths.
- **Add Basic Guest Facilities** - Toilets, a drink stall and a food stall are the most important so make sure to add these.
- **An Exhibit** - A dual exhibit is a good starter as one keep can manage this and a habitat.
- **A Habitat** - Make sure to balance costs and appeal.
- **Donation Bin** - Add these where guests congregate.
- **Paths, Benches and Bins** - You should add these to increase guest comfort.
- **Hire Staff** - A keeper, vet, caretaker, and mechanic are most vital. You can add security and guides later.
- Once these basics are in place expand slowly as your funds allow.

A BEGINNERS GUIDE TO HABITATS, EXHIBITS AND ANIMAL CARE

Preparing Habitat Animals

Animals in habitats are the main focus of many career zoos in particular, so getting these right is essential. The best way to do this is to use the animal information you can access by clicking on them.

After a while, you'll become more aware of the needs of common animals but to begin with, the easiest way to start is to build a reasonable size habitat and simply add an animal into it. Putting your animal into quarantine before moving them into an exhibit can help prevent issues but isn't essential. When you are just starting out there is less risk, especially if you only have one animal. However, when adding an extra animal at a later time, it becomes more essential to make sure they aren't bringing in a contagious disease.

To build a basic exhibit you just need a fence. While open fences allow visitors to see more if the entire fence is open it can cause animals distress. A good choice for a starting fence is the log barrier. It's cheap, you can add glass to specific panels to create viewing areas, and you can add anti-climb barriers if required. The habitat overlay is helpful here to identity if animals will be able to escape your enclosure.

Once the animal is in the exhibit and unboxed, you can pause the game to stop any negative effects of the inappropriate environment while you sort it out. Simply click on the animal and you'll see their information displayed in a window with different tabs.

Getting The Essentials Right

The window you see in the screenshot above is your blueprint for getting the correct habitat. If you follow the prompts on each tab you can't go wrong. However, it's worth noting that you don't need to make everything optimal to keep welfare high.

Start with the terrain and focus on this first. The terrain has a huge effect on the welfare of your animals and is the easiest and cheapest way to make a habitat appropriate. Therefore it's worth taking the time to experiment with the terrain paint to ensure each of the terrain bars is green.

You'll also need to make sure you add a food and water source as well as a shelter. The navigable area section will tell you if an animal requires swimming space or climbing space and if the habitat is too small.

Once this screen looks green, as in the above screenshot, the main part is done. You can now move onto foliage and enrichment.

Adding The Extras

Once you click the foliage tab you'll see a list of the continents and biomes appropriate for the animal in your exhibit. Use these to filter the foliage and then place trees, plants, or bushes as required.

As soon as the bar for coverage hits green you can stop. Often this can be as little as one to two pieces of greenery. While most animals will tolerate more, this isn't essential and can be added later.

The other additions are enrichment items but often these will have to be researched. It's a good idea to try and research the initial level of each animal as soon as you can so you can at least add some enrichment to their habitats. It's also worth checking what other animals unlocked enrichment items are suitable for as there is often overlap. For instance, all big cats will have very similar enrichment needs.

Exhibit Animals

Exhibit animals are the easiest to care for and can attract a large crowd. You simply need to add them to the exhibits and make sure you set the correct temperature and humidity, as shown on the animal's welfare tab.

Once this is done, research will unlock extra items you can add to the exhibits to increase welfare. While not essential, it will raise welfare significantly, even just adding one option, and doesn't cost anything.

Most prebuilt animal exhibits come with display screens for education. Sell the ones you don't need for a refund then make sure you set the others to show information for the correct animal.

Ongoing Care

All animals will need zookeepers to make regular visits to them in order to replenish food, water, and clean the exhibit or habitat. There are a few things you can do to make this process more efficient. These are setting work zones, placing keeper huts in accessible places, and making sure visits are frequent.

You can make visits more efficient by grouping exhibits in small clusters and adding a keeper hut and staff room in a central location. We recommend a small keeper hut for one to two keepers and a large one for three to four. This minimizes staff's waiting time and the amount of time they spend walking around. If you see a lot of queueing notifications you can add an extra hut where required.

Work zones will also ensure animals are visited properly. We recommend starting by setting up two exhibits along with the closest keeper hut and staff room per keeper and keeping an eye on their workload. Some animals, especially those in large herds, are more work than others and may require one keeper just to maintain their habitat, while others can be grouped together. While setting up work zones don't forget to add your exhibits as these also require keeper attention and can be easy to miss. It's also good to have an extra keeper with no work zone who can fill in the gaps caused by other keepers' breaks.

Using the water pumps or placing small pools of water can also help since these will not require frequent replenishment, meaning animals always have access to drinking water. However, water placed as part of the terrain will require a water filtration unit placed within range or will need replacing once it gets dirty, to avoid any diseases entering your enclosure.

Maintaining Standards

Once you've set up the enclosures, work zones, and paths the main thing you need to do is keep an eye on your notifications to head off any issues that crop up. The most common problems are diseases, hygiene, and food or water issues. You may also encounter fights, inbreeding, and injuries.

Infected or injured animals can be clicked on and sent to quarantine, or have a vet attend to them immediately. This is essential to stop the illness from spreading. A shortage of food or water or a dirty habitat is usually a keeper issue but can be a layout problem. If a habitat requires a lot of cleaning then it may need a keeper assigned just to that one location. If food or water is running low try increasing the size or number of food bowls and ensure they are all accessible. You can also add water pumps to keep a better supply of freshwater. Watch your animals and check they can eat or drink from them.

If you have issues with inbreeding, fights, or overcrowding then selling or releasing animals is the answer. Sometimes with small groups of animals, it may be required to replace one of your breeding age animals, or to apply contraception to prevent younger animals from inbreeding once they age up.

If you have a good setup from the start and keep an eye on your population, most issues can be prevented before they even crop up.

If you want more help with your zoo planning make sure to check out our other Planet Zoo articles.

GUIDES

MAINTAINING ANIMAL WELFARE WHILE MAXIMIZING PROFIT

Use The Zoopedia

If you're short on cash then a great first step is to head over to the Zoopedia before you make any purchases. Some animals will require huge amounts of space, while others will need extreme temperatures that have to be maintained with heaters or coolers, depending on your zoo's climate. Certain species also have requirements for climbable or swimmable space.

If you look up different animals you can see the space, biome, and temperature requirements for them. This can help you work out how expensive an optimal exhibit will be to produce. It's also worth bearing in mind that creating climbing space can be a nightmare if you don't have any climbing blueprints unlocked. Sometimes trees will count, for instance, the bare trees suitable for Red Panda exhibits, but mostly you'll need to build platforms and that can be very fiddly. Using a mechanic to unlock the first set of blueprints through research is advisable early on for this reason.

Balance Cost And Appeal

While some animals are very cheap to keep happy if they aren't appealing they won't draw in the visitors and earn you those top donations. For this reason, it's a good idea to look at the most appealing animals you have access to and work out which you can build habitats for most easily. Exhibit animals can also help here since they can be very appealing and the costs of keeping them are small.

Red Pandas are a fantastic crowd puller that is manageable early on as they don't require as much investment in their habitat as some other appealing species. Snakes are often the most appealing exhibit animal type and you can keep them either alone or in pairs.

Whichever animals you choose, make sure that you place donation tubs in the places you see visitors gathering to admire them. Adding educational screens and speakers can also encourage visitors to stay longer and become more likely to throw some money in the tub.

Sell Your Young

Ok, this sounds harsh but hear us out. Overcrowded exhibits are bad for animals so you do need to keep an eye on the numbers. You also need to watch out for inbreeding, although this will usually generate an alert so you can stop it.

Certain animals will breed frequently and selling or releasing their young into the wild will earn you enough money or conservation credits to purchase more animals and expand your zoo and in turn your profit.

Japanese Macaques are cheap crowd-pleasers that breed well and mature quickly. Flamingos are similar but can be overwhelming since they breed very fast and like to live in large groups. For those happy to wait, Nile Monitors take a while to age but earn a large number of conservation points once released. Cheetahs are also a good investment being cheap to feed and producing up to five cubs per birth.

In terms of exhibit animals, small creatures such as spiders and beetles often breed frequently. You'll need to keep an eye on them though, as their numbers increase fast and can overcrowd an exhibit quickly. They won't sell for much but you will have a frequent supply of excess insects.

Combine Species

Certain species can live in groups with others. This is a great way to increase the number of habitat animals without having to build new enclosures. Zebras or Common Warthogs are especially good for this as they can live with each other as well as several other species including Springboks, Sable Antelopes, and Reticulated Giraffes.

Just make sure you check on the animal's welfare as sometimes just because you can, doesn't mean you should. For example, while Ostrichs can also live with Zebras, the speed at which they run around an enclosure can stress out other animals. You'll also need to keep expanding the space as the number of animals increases, especially if you add Giraffes, as these have a huge space requirement.

Use The Terrain

You can use the terrain to make more natural enclosures and in some cases, it can be used in place of fencing. Large cliffs or rivers with steep banks can help keep animals where you need them to be, without needing to fully enclose them with a fence. You can also make caves to act as a shelter, which is especially handy with larger herds as it can save space and money.

All you need to do is complete your fencing with the null barrier, which has no cost, and make sure the edges are just outside of where the animals can get to. This will ensure that the terrain overlay will show you accurately where any escape points are.

To ensure visitors can still see you can build viewing platforms over the terrain, allowing them to look down into the enclosure. Just make sure you have some space where you can place a fence on flat ground, in order to add a door for the keepers to enter the enclosure.

Encourage Spending And Donating

Happy animals will encourage visitors but there are other things you can do to ensure your visitors stick around and spend more time and money at your zoo. The main one is to make sure their needs are met. This means providing food, drink, and restrooms. These things are usually profitable by themselves but when you start out using vending machines instead of shops to avoid the vendor staffing cost can be beneficial. Vending machines are also great for lesser-visited areas of the zoo to ensure needs can still be maintained even further away from the main hub.

Education is another crowd puller and adding screens and speakers will encourage visitors. Hosting animal talks will also attract crowds, especially to exhibits that have a high appeal and where the educators are able to feed the animals during the talk. Make sure that these facilities have donation tubs close by so visitors can show their appreciation with cash.

Well placed ATMS will ensure visitors can spend more and donation tubs situated on the exit path can also be surprisingly lucrative. To check you've got donation tubs in the right place click on them regularly to see how much has gone into them.

It's also beneficial to guide your visitors. Adding viewing platforms or small sections where animals are visible through fences can help ensure that donation tubs are placed where people are gathering. Making some of the fences non-transparent will also increase animal welfare and reduce stress. Just make sure that the viewing areas do offer good views. Zoo patrons will be quick to tell you if they don't, so keep an eye on guest thoughts.

If you want more help with your zoo planning make sure to check out our other Planet Zoo articles.

TIPS FOR TIMED SCENARIOS

Check Your Game Settings

Time is of the essence here and the challenges are based on real-time, rather than in-game time. This means that tweaking your game settings can make a huge difference. If you have an older or lower spec computer you may need to set your graphics details or guest numbers a little lower while you build to avoid lag slowing you down. Then simply ramp them up to get that loan paid off.

The speed of your game will also make a difference. Full speed can help money generate faster to meet financial goals but this can lead to management issues. Balancing the settings will be the key to success.

Make A Plan

Knowing what your goals are is essential to success. You don't want to waste time on aspects of the game that aren't required. Having the goals always visible can be helpful for keeping your focus.

It's also good to make a plan. Work out which parts of management and building are most essential or take the longest to achieve and get these in place first. Do you need to earn money? Build your park rating? Improve animal welfare? Once you have goals prioritized it's easier to know where to put your resources and in what order.

Don't Be Afraid To Restart

The Australia scenario in particular requires a specific number of animals and exhibits. Due to the way the Animal Trading Market works you may find it is more beneficial to restart your scenario in order to get a better combination of animals.

Mistakes early on can also lead to bigger errors later and starting again after half an hour can be more beneficial than limping on for another hour before failing.

Use Prebuilt Facilities To Save Time

Since speed is essential, the prebuilt guest and staff facilities will save you a huge amount of time. Building can be both fiddly and time-consuming so placing pre-built solutions will be beneficial.

The themed pre-builds will give you a good approval rating quickly and you can even sell odd pieces back later to raise money if required, especially on the final push.

Mix Species When Possible

Speed may be essential but space, especially in the regular timed scenario, can be limited. Combining species can save both time and space since you'll only need to make one exhibit but gain the appeal, welfare, and space benefits of having two.

Just make sure you know which species will live together well. Finding out you made a mistake in regards to this after you combined the animals won't end well for anyone.

Use Vending Machines And Shops

Guests require their needs fulfilling to stay happy and using a mix of shops and the new vending machines helps with this. Placing vending machines on the odd paths in areas where shops won't fit can help boost needs more easily.

Just remember that you'll also need toilets to keep your guests happy so prioritize these when space is sparse.

Take Out Loans To Ramp Up Fast

If you have long term goals that require maintaining ratings or profits over time it can be beneficial to take out a loan to get your infrastructure in place quicker. Prioritize essentials we well as animals that will draw in guests.

You need to double-check your goals and build to your priorities. If you've got them right the zoo should be making a profit that can be used to ditch the loan while also making a growing income over time, thus hitting two types of financial goals at once.

Don't Neglect Welfare

You'll need to make sure you keep an eye on both animal and staff welfare. Overcrowding of animals due to breeding will not only make them unhappy but it also reduces income as these extra animals can be sold for money or released for conservation points.

Staff also need to be kept happy as if they quit and you miss the notification you'll end up with all kinds of issues that affect your park rating and other factors relating to your goals.

Use Your Work Zones

Work zones do take a little time to set up but using them efficiently will make sure your zoo can run more efficiently at a fast speed, saving time overall. As long as everything is covered and your staff levels are correct this will be your biggest boost to efficient running.

Having a well-run zoo in place as you build will help you focus on the specific goals, rather than worrying about little problems constantly cropping up.

Remember The Extras

The extras are what will make your zoo. Here we're talking about bins to keep litter under control, donation tubs for increased profits, and education boards for guests to enjoy. It's also beneficial to ensure viewing platforms are optimal for both guests and animals.

It's also easy to miss benches, lighting, decor and other similar tiny touches but especially if you have appeal based goals then these will be important.

If you want more help with your zoo planning make sure to check out our other Planet Zoo articles.

GUIDE TO CREATING THE PERFECT PENGUIN ENCLOSURE

Building The Basics

The first step in building a penguin enclosure is making space for the water. While you can do this by lowering the terrain I found it easier to raise it and have the underwater viewing area come in at ground level.

Penguins need a clear four-meter depth of water so it's a good idea to ensure your terrain is raised by more than this, otherwise, you'll need to dig down in the middle later on. The easiest way to ensure a good body of water visitors can see into is by creating a horseshoe shape in the terrain as shown above.

The next step is to add the barrier that will enclose your exhibit.

There are a couple of things to note here in order to get the barrier to place properly. The main one is that you must start building the barrier from the highest point on the terrain. This means it will properly extend down to the ground where the gaps are.

You also need to make sure you've selected a waterproof fence and we recommend the setting that keeps the top of the barrier at the same height but allows the bottom to be edited. This is because if you adjust any terrain inside the exhibit to smooth it out of similar you may need to adjust the barrier to prevent issues with the water.

If the fence appears to have come away from the terrain, simply click on the fence post and use the arrow keys to pull it down and close the gap. This will ensure that the water will still place properly in the exhibit.

Once the barrier is set up it's time to make sure the guests and keepers have access to the area.

Add The Access

This path gives visitors a place to see the animals both above and below the water. It can be fiddly to set up, since the paths on the ground and those that are raised up like to try and link together by default.

I found the easiest way was to create the path across the top of the two sides of the horseshoe by the barrier first. This will then connect itself down to the main length of the path on the ground. Then you can delete the high-level straight path to prevent it from trying to connect as stairs to the bottom. The bottom path is a circle (ish, I'm sure more patience would produce a better job) and once this is complete you can simply add the top path back in. You can also turn off the align to placement setting but this can make the staircases harder to place.

If you're struggling a little with the mouse controls the keyboard shortcuts can be helpful. These are the most useful:

- Raise or Lower Path (without placing) - U and J
- Adjust Vertical Height - Shift and Arrows/Mouse
- Adjust Path Length - = and -
- Adjust Path Width - [and]
- Path T Junction - X
- Create Y Junction - Hold Z while making a junction
- Toggle Curved Slopes On/Off - V
- Toggle Align To Placement Suggestions On/Off - B

Once your paths are in place make sure you add the keeper door and access paths in the same way.

Making The Habitat Suitable

The easiest way to ensure the habitat is suitable is to add the animal, click them to bring up their information tab then pause the game. You can navigate the tabs along the top of the info panel to find the correct terrain, plant, and space requirements.

The sliders for both plants and terrain will change while the game is paused, although it needs to be in live mode to assess the water, space, and climbable space requirements.

For the King Penguin, you need to change the terrain in two steps to ensure it's all correct. You can see above that the first step was adding the water into the space we created earlier. Since it is more than four-meters deep you can see that the navigable space, swimmable space, and deep water requirements are all met.

The main requirement for the King Penguin that's not as immediately obvious is the cold temperature requirement. You can find the temperature information in the Zoopedia entry for each animal.

You'll need to place some coolers and set them to around -18, which is in the middle of the preferred temperature range you can see in the image above.

In terms of terrain, the penguin requires mostly sand, soil, and short grass. You can use any combination you like since the specific percentages of each are far more flexible than most animals.

Once these are in place and the coolers are set, add snow to the exhibit for a more authentic feel and to keep those penguins happy.

Finishing Touches

King Penguins don't actually want or need plants and trees but they will tolerate a couple so it's worth adding them to enhance the look of the exhibit. You'll also need to make sure you add the essentials for food and water.

King Penguins don't need an extra water source but there is an underwater feeder that provides feeding enrichment. You'll notice that there's also a small feeding tray on the ground in the image above. This was added in case zookeepers have issues routing to the underwater feeder on occasion.

Penguins also love other enrichment items including the new floating platform and rubber duck you can see above. You can also add bubble machines or sprinklers.

TIPS FOR BREEDING PERFECT ANIMALS

Keep Their Welfare High

A happy animal is prepared to mate with other animals, and this is just one reason to keep your animal's welfare as high as it can possibly go. This means buying better food, keeping them well fed, adding new toys into their enclosures, and creating a habitat they enjoy.

Even when they are first starting out, beginners can make their animals decently happy with the items that are given to them.

Research Breeding

A vet can perform research on a specific animal, which in turn can increase their breeding statistics. It will not only raise their overall welfare, but it will also help their fertility numbers to make it easier to breed them.

This will also help you to raise their overall stats as well as you continue to work to create the perfect specimen.

Maximize The Number Of Potential Offspring

You can maximize the number of potential offspring by pairing a male with as many females as he can handle. Some species have one mate, while others can impregnate multiple females at once.

Look at the Zoopedia and study the animal to see how you can adjust your current animals to give yourself a chance at the largest number of offspring possible.

Your Primary Focus Should Be On Size And Longevity

There are four main aspects to their genetics, not including color and pattern, and they are size, longevity, immunity, and fertility. The ones that you can easily change are size and longevity, which is why this should be your first focus.

Once you have managed to max out the size and longevity of a few animals, then you can begin to look at the other stats.

Utilize The Trade Center As Storage

The Trade Center is where all the animals you purchase are sent, but it is also a great place to store those animals that you plan to use for breeding. Once you begin to have animals that are genetically great, they can then be transferred to this building until you are ready to use them.

It is also a way to save money as both their needs and age will be frozen, so you don't have to worry about them aging out of their breeding window too quickly.

Inbreeding Will Decrease Your Stats

The best way to ruin your chances of breeding genetically perfect animals is to inbreed them. This means that your parent animals have offspring with their children, which never ends well, and it is why the Indian Peafowl is not one of the best to start off with.

It can lead to future offspring with poor genetics, even if the child has amazing genetics of its own. The most often outcome is a lack of fertility, which will decrease your conservation credits and sale price when you decide to move the animal out of your zoo.

Apply Contraception To Any Offspring

One pro tip to preventing this inbreeding from happening is to apply contraception to any of the parent's offspring. This will prevent any accidents from happening as you decide what direction to take with your breeding program. The contraception can be found in your zoo's animal management page on the right side of the screen.

It looks like a pill, and players can tell when it is applied because the bar turns red. Players might not think they need it, but after your turtles have thousands of offspring in mere minutes, they tend to change their stance on the topic.

Keep The Best Offspring

The goal when breeding better animals is not to keep every single baby that your animal has. You should aim to keep the animal with the best genetics, or even one with a gold, silver, or bronze ribbon. It is easy to figure out which is the best by clicking on each offspring and looking at their genetics chart.

The more green that the animal has on their chart, the better its genetics. Players can be tempted to sell off these amazing animals for extra cash or conservation credits, but this tends to work negatively against them once the parents die off and they are left with nothing.

Create Several Enclosures

Some players like to breed multiple pairs of animals in the same zoo, so they create numerous enclosures for the same species, and many are based on existing zoos. This way they can continue to breed their original pair, as well as the offspring, to try and create the best animal possible through multiple pairs.

Other players even start with two pairs of a species and then breed their best offspring once they have matured. It opens more doors and it is often the best option for those who want to focus on this aspect of the game.

Compare Their Genetics

If you are unsure if one of your animals is the offspring of another, you can always compare them using the genetics chart. It even allows you to switch out the parent animals so you can find the best pair to breed.

If you have multiple great animals, this chart will help you decide which one to consider for a parent as you see the gene potential of the offspring they could have. This is the most useful tool the game gives you in regards to this area, so any breeder should be ready to pull this up regularly.

Create Family Charts

If you want to go all out and are determined to make the best breeding program possible, then you should make a chart outside of the game.

A genealogy chart was added to the game for players to use, but some still find it easier to make their own in order to create a breeding plan.

You could use a spreadsheet, paper, or even post-it notes to create the perfect species. Players use multiple different tells within their charts to indicate life, death, and generation.

- **Choose The Alpha**

Some species in the game have an alpha male, female, or both, and they are the only ones of that gender who breed. It is usually the female with better genetics who wins this prestigious status, but not always.

If you find the wrong animal is your alpha, then you can trade them out of the zoo to keep the right animal in charge. The alpha status is shown in the individual animal menu. It is located at the top on the first page with their overall stats next to the gender symbol.

- **Sell Or Release Male Offspring**

Many animals in the game are in promiscuous relationships, which means they aren't monogamous with a single mate and it is something beginners often don't realize. It is easier in these situations to trade or release the males to the wild, as there is usually only one in these types of enclosures.

This system works because it decreases the number of great animals you need to find on the market as you only have to find one, rather than five. If your female ends up being better than your male offspring, it can be a difficult decision, but it is best to stick with the female.

Know Which Gender Is On The Market

It is not uncommon for certain genders to be more plentiful on the marketplace due to one being worth more than the other. This problem is prominent in franchise mode, as people hope to gain more conservation credits from their sale.

Many times the males are the more expensive animal to purchase, so this could alter your breeding plans. If it is too hard to find one gender of an animal, then consider keeping the other.

Use Letters To Label New Generations

A pro tip that many players have found useful is to start labeling their offspring with letters. The parents are usually given an 'A' and then their offspring are given a 'B' and so on.

It helps players keep track of whose offspring is whose based on their generation within the game so they can put more focus into their custom creations.

If you want more help with your zoo planning make sure to check out our other Planet Zoo articles.

PRO TIPS EVERY PLAYER SHOULD KNOW

Keep It Simple

As soon as the game starts it can be tempting as a new player to spend every penny you have to build as many habitats as possible and buy some of the more profitable animals. The problem with this is you don't have a whole lot of money in the beginning and the more profitable animals are also the more problematic, especially if you don't have enough resources to deal with them.

Stick to simple animals like Tortoises that will generate steady profits and help you build a good foundation. As your finances and reputation start growing you can slowly ramp up into bigger enclosures and more interesting animals.

⁜ Share Habitat Space

One thing you can do to keep it simple in the beginning and to minimize your costs is to have animals share space. Obviously you only want compatible animals sharing an enclosure otherwise you might see injuries and other problems.

Additional benefits from sharing habitats is that some animals will be happier with their roommates and guests appreciate not having to travel far to see a variety of animals. Your staff won't have to travel far to maintain the habitat either which will keep them happy.

⁜ Loans Are For Profit

Loans can be a powerful tool for growing your zoo quickly, but if done improperly can cause you to be perpetually low on funds or even closing your doors. The only reason you should ever take out a loan is if you are building/buying something that is guaranteed to generate a profit equal to or greater than what the loan will cost.

Many players will take out a loan to cover repairs if they're low on cash and this is a very, very bad idea. Keep an emergency fund for these kinds of problems and maintenance issues and use loans to generate profit.

⁜ Manage Loan Payments

If you made a mistake with your loans or what you used it on isn't as profitable as you anticipated, then you can lower your payments to give yourself some more wiggle room. This will increase the overall amount you spend to pay off your loan, but it does free up some cash flow which you can use to make profits.

As your finances start improving and you begin making more money increase your loan payments accordingly and get them paid off as quickly as possible. Remember, loans are for profits, cash is for emergencies.

Souvenirs And Donations

One way to increase your cash flow is to motivate guests to spend money inside the zoo. Unfortunately, and understandably, guests aren't very inclined to spend money and will often walk away without spending anything other than the price of admission.

The two best ways to get something more from guests are donation boxes and merchandise shops. For whatever reason these seem to be the best money makers for the best cost. So if you're between building projects and want to squeeze some more funds from your guests then start littering your zoo with these.

Don't Waste Credits

It's also important you properly budget your Conservation Credits. This currency is extremely valuable and can buy some great things, but early on you wont have an efficient way to generate them and will regret spending them right away, especially on things that can be bought with cash.

Stick to cash in the beginning and once you have some things setup and Conservation Credits start flowing into your wallet then you can be a little more liberal with how you spend them.

Breed And Release

One way to get more Conservation Credits is to buy animals with cash, breed them, raise the offspring to be happy and healthy, then release them into the wild in exchange for Conservation Credits. If you sell them you only get cash, you must release them into the wild to get Credits.

Once you have enough Credits you can buy more exotic animals that will then breed and produce offspring you can sell or release for Credits. But in the mean time hold onto your Credits, breed simpler animals, and release them for easy Credits.

More Females Than Males

As you begin your large-scale breeding operation keep track of how many males you have in each habitat. For many species too many males in a single habitat will start fights which leads to injuries, upset gusts, and more work for your staff.

When you start getting too many males consider releasing or selling them off to keep the peace. Don't accidentally get rid of all your males as you still need a few for breeding, but don't be afraid to have skewed ratios between males and females. If things are still getting out of hand you can use contraceptions to keep the populations in line.

Have The Right Staff Balance

Now that your zoo is growing and more guests are showing up it's important to ensure you have the right staff to animal to guest ratios. Too few Keepers will result in dirty habitats and unhappy animals, too few Vets will result in too many sick animals, and a lack of Security Guards will cause unruly guests to take over and cause problems.

You want a good balance of staff to keep everything inline that still fits within your monthly budget. If you are careful with finances and have a good foundation of animals then hiring staff to meet your needs shouldn't be a problem.

Give Employees Their Own Space

Unlike animals the staff likes to have their own space. A staff member can't share a small facility space with another and this causes one to stand outside waiting while the other finishes whatever they're doing. Make sure to build a lot of small facility areas until you can get into the larger spaces that can be shared.

It's also a good idea to route areas for staff to use. Not only will this allow them to respond to problems faster and more efficiently they wont be forced to wade through crowds which isn't good for them or the guests.

HOW TO BUILD A HARD SHELTER

What Is A Hard Shelter?

In Planet Zoo, a hard shelter is one that provides a solid roof above your animals' heads. This is opposed to open or soft shelter, which is when you place your animal bedding outside or underneath a natural canopy.

What Type Of Shelter Do Animals Need?

Your animals will need a certain minimum amount of hard shelter within their enclosure, and you can find the level required of each by clicking on one of them to open the animal information box. Then go to **Welfare > Habitat > Hard Shelter**.

For this to be 100 percent, the hard shelter in the enclosure must be able to cover all of your animals in their entirety, so different sized animals will need a different amount. Elephants would for example, obviously, need a lot, whereas Meerkats need less.

You can make a hard shelter in one of two ways: the easy, but slightly ugly, way of buying one directly from the **Habitat Menu** (under the **Shelter Tab**), or by making your own using the landscaping tools. Both of these methods will increase the **Hard Shelter** percentage in the same way, so there's no real benefit to one or the other apart from the aesthetics, but you may also be able to save a few pennies on the pre-built structures if you are efficient with your landscaping.

How To Build Your Own Hard Shelter With The Landscaping Tools

Building your own shelter means that you can better blend it into the habitat you've made, make it more visually appealing, and also make something that suits the biome that your animal is used to. For example, a rocky, cave-like shelter can look especially good for mountainous animal habitats. So, it's a good idea to try and use them where and when you can.

Here's how to do it:

- Select the **Terrain** icon, then click the **Terrain Stamp** tool. This is the second button down in the list of options. Select a stamp shape (you can use any of them, depending on the style you'd like the shelter to be in), then adjust the height and width. Clicking on any patch of ground after selecting the **Terrain Stamp** tool will now landscape an area to the exact specifications of the stamp you just made.

- Once you have created your terrain shape, select the **Sculpting** tool (the topmost button in the list), then the **Push** button. Adjust the **Push** sizes and intensity to taste, then click, hold, and drag on the stamped terrain shape to make a cave shape into it. Play around with this to make the shape of the shelter the way you'd like, and make sure to create a reasonably sized flat surface in the centre (you can use the **Flatten To Surface** tool to help with this).

- Go to the **Habitat** menu, then **Beds and Shelters**. Select a bed that is of a size appropriate for the animal that will be using it, then place the bed in the middle of the shelter you just made. After this, there's only one more step.

↓ **Checking The Hard Shelter's Coverage**

Once the bedding has been placed inside your shelter, you will need to check the shelter's coverage so that your animals are safely tucked up out of the wind, rain, and snow.

You do this by clicking on the **Bedding** you've just placed, then looking at the info box in the top right of the screen. If the shelter status is **Exposed**, then it is not covered properly, even if it looks like it is. If this happens, try expanding the shelter a little using the terrain tools, then check the status again. Keep expanding it until it changes to dry.

It is possible to landscape around the prefabricated shelters available in the **Habitat Menu** . You can do this if you are struggling to achieve full coverage with a landscaped shelter that is elaborate, or in an awkward spot.

Once the shelter status is **Dry**, and has turned green, then you're good to go – your animals now have a place to snuggle away from the pressures of life without your zoo's guests constantly prying on them!

HOW TO INSTALL AND USE MODS

With all the hundreds upon hundreds of decorations and animals you can choose from in Planet Zoo, you'd think there couldn't possibly be a need for more content. Modders stop at nothing to ensure all players have everything they need, whether that be a new species or creative new habitats.

Modding is made easy with the use of Steam Workshop, but there are other ways to obtain mods as well. Most of Planet Zoo's existing mods won't make the game easier or provide advantages but are instead made to give players more options when it comes to designing their dream zoo. The game may be in the management genre, but the designing aspect of it is a calming and exciting one as well.

There's plenty of mods to choose from, but Planet Zoo also offers up to seven different DLC's. These DLC's provide up to five new animals each, new maps, and over 210 new structures each. They are aimed to take a look at other parts of the world, at animals and climates North American's don't know enough about.

DLC's:

- South American
- Southeast Asia
- Arctic
- Africa
- Australia

Installing Mods With Steam Workshop

Planet Zoo has Steam Workshop support. If you own the game on Steam instead of another platform, this is the absolute easiest way to apply mods. By going to the game in your Steam Library, there will be multiple headings under the Play button such as Store, Discussions, and Workshop. Another way to get to the Steam Workshop page is to hover over the Community tab in Steam and click Workshop, then search for Planet Zoo.

To download mods from the Workshop, all you have to do is find something you like and then press Subscribe. The moment you subscribe to a mod using Steam Workshop, it's instantly installed into your game. It only takes one second for Steam to access the correct Planet Zoo files and enable any Workshop mods available.

The most popular mods on Steam Workshop are habitats. Modders create unique habitats and stores for different themes and animals. These can be animal structures made for different species' specific needs like climbing, pretty kiosks for customer use, or extravagant decorations for all-around use.

Notable Steam Workshop mods:

- Zooton Tower
- Reptile Centre
- Pride Rock
- Biomimic Learning Center
- Green Path Tunnel

Installing Mods With Nexus Mods

Getting your Planet Zoo mods from Nexus Mods takes a little bit more work. It's not an instant connection to your copy of the game. Instead, you have to manually place mod files into the Planet Zoo files on your computer to get everything to work.

Most mods for Planet Zoo on Nexus Mods are new animal species. It will be hard to do anything else, as this is where animal mods are most frequent as opposed to large structures from Steam Workshop. If you have a favorite type of animal that isn't in Planet Zoo or that you need to purchase DLC for, Nexus Mods has got your back.

To install new species from this website, you first have to find one you like, then click Files instead of Description. Here, you will need to **click Manual Download**.

You **can't download mods from Nexus Mods unless you have an account** with them and are logged in.

Once the file is downloaded, you must **find your "ovldata" folder in your Planet Zoo files**. The easiest way to find this is by right-clicking Planet Zoo in your Steam inventory and clicking Properties. Press Local Files and then Browse. From here, type "ovldata" in the search bar. Click the folder that pops up. Now all you have to do is **extract the file** of the mod you just downloaded into this ovldata folder and voila.

Notable Nexus Mods mods:

- North American River Otter
- Eurasian Lynx
- Rocky Mountain Elk
- Alpaca
- American Black Bear

Enabling and Using Mods In Planet Zoo

Once you've extracted the mod file using Nexus Mods or Subscribed to an item using Steam Workshop, your new mod will automatically be in the game. There's actually nothing else you need to do! Just find the item in-game by searching through the category it would be in.

For instance, if you downloaded a new turtle habitat, go into Nature in Planet Zoo like you normally would and use the search bar or scroll to find the habitat. If you downloaded a new species, go into Animal Trading and search or scroll until you find the animal.

Installing mods in Planet Zoo is made easy and efficient by both the modders and the platforms you can use. You can have unique and custom structures and animals for use in your zoo in no time.

FAQ GUIDE

- **Which Consoles Is Planet Zoo: Console Edition Available On?**

Planet Zoo: Console Edition is available on the **Xbox Series S|X** as well as **PlayStation 5**.

- **What Editions Are Available, And What Do They Include?**

There are **three different versions** of Planet Zoo: Console Edition. They are Regular, Deluxe, and Ultimate. Each one includes all the content from the smaller editions.

Planet Zoo: Console Edition

This **base game edition** has everything you need to get started in your zoo management career. It contains all **72 base game animals**, and **four game modes**: career mode, franchise mode, challenge mode and sandbox mode.

Planet Zoo: Deluxe Edition

The deluxe edition is available as a standalone add-on, or bundled with the base game. It adds **16 new animals from the Wetlands and Southeast Asia**, as well as **two new campaign scenarios**.

Wetlands Animals	Southeast Asian Animals
Capybara	Sun Bear

Wetlands Animals	Southeast Asian Animals
Platypus	Clouded Leopard
Asian Small-Clawed Otter	Malaysian Tapir
Spectacled Caiman	Proboscis Monkey
Nile Lechwe	North Sulawesi Babirusa
Wild Water Buffalo	Binturong
Red-Crowned Crane	Ussuri Dhole
Danube Crested Newt	Giant Leaf Insect

The first scenario sees you managing **Green Leaf Zoological,** which is situated in the Brazilian Pantanal, the world's largest wetland. The second takes place in Perek, Malaysia where you must turn a profit at **Kuala Bintu Taman**, surrounded by beautiful tropical rainforest.

Planet Zoo Console Edition: Ultimate Edition

This edition features **everything in the Deluxe Edition as well as the upcoming Season Pass,** which will comprise 14 DLC packs. These add **81 animals, 15 campaign scenarios, and over 2000 new scenery items** to the game.

The Season Pass content will be released in stages between launch and March 31, 2025.

⊥ **How Much Does Planet Zoo Console Edition Cost?**

The price will vary depending on the store and edition you purchase. The RRP for each is as follows:

- **Base Game:** £39.99/$49.99/€49.99
- **Deluxe Edition:** £49.99/$59.99/€59.99
- **Ultimate Edition:** £99.99/$119.99/€119.99

Prices may vary depending on the storefront you use.

- Can You Buy A Physical Edition Of Planet Zoo: Console?

There are currently **no plans to release a physical version of the game.** All copies are digital download codes.

- Does Planet Zoo Console Edition Include All The Updates Made To The PC Version?

Almost. **All PC updates from the first four years,** including 15 feature updates and many quality of life adjustments, currently bring the console edition almost up to date.

Update 16, which was released for PC on December 13, 2023, and includes modular souvenir stores, four new music tracks, and some foliage, **will be coming shortly after launch.** The third anniversary free animal, the **Collared Peccary will also be added** soon.

- Will Planet Zoo: Console Edition Include All The DLC On PC?

After launch, **14 DLC packs will be available over time.** These will be purchasable individually or as part of the Season Pass that comes with the Ultimate Edition. The Season Pass content will be released over the next year and completed by March 31, 2025.

- Is Planet Zoo: Console Edition Multiplayer?

As with the PC version, **there is no multiplayer zoo gameplay in Planet Zoo: Console Edition.** However, you can **trade animals with other players in Franchise Mode**, and share your zoo creations with the community using the **Frontier Workshop.**

- **Is Planet Zoo: Console Edition Cross Platform?**

Partly. **Trading on the Animal Market in Franchise mode is only available with players on the same platform.** However, the **Frontier Workshop is cross-platform**, allowing you to share and download creations from across the entire console community.

- **What Are The Differences Between The PC And Console Versions?**

The Console Edition has been **optimized for controller use and also console performance.** The **menus have been redesigned** to allow them to be more intuitive to navigate with a controller, but the same information is still included.

You'll also see a **Complexity Meter** in the console version. As your zoo becomes more detailed, this will keep track of how much needs to be loaded as you navigate the zoo. The higher this number, the more performance issues you may encounter.

This lets you decide if you want to sacrifice a little visual fidelity for that complex custom store you dreamed of, and also easily keep an eye on how different items can affect performance without having to make guesses.

- **Will Planet Zoo Console Edition Support Keyboard and Mouse?**

Yes. While you will still be using the controller-friendly menus, **if you prefer the keyboard and mouse support for this is included.**

www.ingramcontent.com/pod-product-compliance
Lightning Source LLC
Chambersburg PA
CBHW070409230526
45471CB00006B/2712